M000307389

This Do In Remembrance of Me

THIS DO IN
REMEMBRANCE OF ME

Dr. Douglas D. Feaver

AMBASSADOR INTERNATIONAL
GREENVILLE, SOUTH CAROLINA & BELFAST, NORTHERN IRELAND

www.emeraldhouse.com

THIS DO IN REMEMBRANCE OF ME
© 2008 Douglas D. Feaver
All rights reserved

Printed in the United States of America

ISBN 978-1-932307-68-9

Cover Design & Page Layout by David Siglin of A&E Media

AMBASSADOR INTERNATIONAL
Emerald House
427 Wade Hampton Blvd.
Greenville, SC 29609, USA
www.emeraldhouse.com

AMBASSADOR PUBLICATIONS
Providence House
Ardenlee Street
Belfast, BT6 8QJ
Northern Ireland, UK
www.ambassador-productions.com

This book is published in association with
Patti M. Hummel, President & Agent
The Benchmark Group LLC, Nashville, TN
benchmarkgroup1@aol.com

DEDICATION

I dedicate this book to my wife, Margaret, my faithful lifetime partner in love and prayer and ministry, and to our children David, John, Ruth, and Peter, with whom we have communed in the service of our Lord and Savior Jesus Christ.

And in loving memory of our son Paul, who is already communing with our Lord face to face.

ACKNOWLEDGEMENTS

Thanks to Sandi Tompkins for her thorough editing and inspired creative input. Thanks to Kay Ben-Avraham and Denise Trio for their collaboration in nurturing the cover layout from concept to reality. Special thanks to Colleen Dente for the artwork of the hands breaking bread.

TABLE OF CONTENTS

Foreword	9
Editor's Notes	13
What's in a Name?	15
Jewish Roots	19
Marriage Feast	21
Celebrating Each Other	24
Two Jews Look at the Last Supper	27
A Night of Betrayal	31
The Body of Christ	34
Two Cups or Four?	37
A Last Supper Exit Poll	40
The First Passover	44
Hezekiah Revives the Passover	47
Foot Washing	51
Two Kinds of Night	54
Our Past, Our Present, Our Future	57
High and Low Church	60
Believing In Jesus	64
The Holy Spirit's Role in Communion	67
Jesus's Prayer for Us	70
Lord's Supper as Proclamation	72
"The Lord's Breakfast?"	75
Almost Obsessive Desire	79
The Missing Lamb	81
Breaking of Bread	84
Cup of the New Covenant	87
A Cup of Thanksgiving	91
"And When They Had Sung a Hymn..."	93

FOREWORD

The small volume you hold in your hands is a treasure chest of inspired writings by Dr. Douglas Feaver on one of the most intimate experiences in the life of a Christian, Holy Communion. In the New Testament letter of James are these remarkable words: "Abraham put his faith in God, and that faith was counted to him as righteousness…and he is called 'God's friend.'" I have known and admired Douglas and his beloved wife, Margaret, for more than thirty years and seen firsthand their devotion and commitment to our Holy God, their inspiring and eloquent witness to the life-saving and atoning work of Jesus Christ, and their passion and joy in the life-giving power of the Holy Spirit. All of this leads me to echo the words of James and say that, for me and so many others, Douglas and Margaret "put their faith in God…and are known to us as 'God's friends.'" As such, Douglas offers us something precious – his prayerful reflections on the mystery of the sacrament at the heart of our faith.

These are Douglas's writings, but God's Spirit speaks to us through His humble servant. These beautiful meditations are paired with some of Douglas's favorite hymn texts. Like the great hymnologist Erik Routley, Douglas understands that the Bible and the hymnal are *companion* volumes. These well-chosen hymn stanzas illuminate and amplify Douglas's own words and enrich our understanding of what he wants us to learn – not just in our heads, but deep in our hearts. With his son John serving as editor, Douglas offers us a great gift: the ability to apprehend what the Apostle Paul called "things beyond our seeing, things beyond our hearing, things beyond our imagining, all prepared by God for those who love Him…"

In one of his greatest poems *Love*, George Herbert describes an extraordinary encounter between Jesus Christ, called Love, and the soul of a reluctant believer invited to the Eucharistic feast. The believer draws back; he knows he is unworthy, full of sin, ungrateful. Love assures this believer that his sins are forgiven and atonement made. The believer relents a bit and says he will come to the table, not quite ready to be the guest of Love, but only His servant. Love insists that we are to be His *guest*; He is the gracious host who cares for and serves all who believe, just as He washed the disciples' feet and served them at that first Lord's Supper. The poem ends with these words: "'You must sit down,' says Love, 'and taste my meat.' So I did sit and eat.'"

When the great English composer Ralph Vaughan Williams set this poem in his *Five Mystical Songs*, the final words are accompanied by a choir singing a Communion hymn set to music that breathes peace, acceptance, forgiveness, and a complete surrender to the unconditional love of Jesus Christ. That same Spirit may be found in this volume, and we shall be ever grateful to this 'friend of God' for sharing it with us. *Soli Deo Gloria*!

GREG FUNFGELD
THE FIRST PRESBYTERIAN CHURCH OF BETHLEHEM
ALL SAINTS DAY, 1 NOVEMBER 2008

EDITOR'S NOTES

O ver the two millennia since Jesus of Nazareth lived on this earth, Christians have celebrated a meal with bread and wine or juice. This tradition is based on accounts in each of the first four books of the New Testament (Matthew, Mark, Luke and John) and in First Corinthians.

At the very least, this meal reminds Christians of the body and blood of Jesus. But there is much more to contemplate about this simple practice.

These meditations were originally given in a community setting by my father, Dr. Douglas D. Feaver. His training as a Classics professor is seen in the careful analyses of Greek and Hebrew word meanings and cultural contexts. His passion for hymns is reflected in the hymn texts which are paired with each meditation. Most of all, his love for the Jesus of Communion shines through each page. May that same love inspire each one who reads and ponders these meditations.

WHAT'S IN A NAME?

What is it that we are doing here today? Why are we gathered together? In front of us is a table displaying several loaves of bread, and little cups of fruit juice. What shall we call it? Some will say: "Ah, we are going to have Communion;" others: "It's the Eucharist." For others it is "The Lord's Table;" for others the "Sacrament of the Table." The Catholics (provided, no doubt, the right protocol is followed) would call it "Mass," and the Orthodox, "Liturgy." Paul called it "the Lord's Supper" and many still call it that — even when it is celebrated in the morning.

> *Christians, sing the incarnation*[1]
> *Of th'eternal Son of God,*
> *Who, to save us, took our nature,*
> *Soul and body, flesh and blood;*
> *God, He saw man's cruel bondage,*

[1] *Christians, Sing the Incarnation*, Ernest E. Dugmore, circa 1870. Selected verses.

Who in death's dark dungeon lay;
Man, He came to fight man's battle,
And for man He won the day.
Alleluia, Alleluia
To th'incarnate Son of God,
Who for man as Man hath conquered
In our own true flesh and blood.

By the way, what did Jesus call it? The Scriptures are clear, even if scholars fuss; He called it a "Passover . . ."

Through a life of lowly labor
He on earth was pleased to dwell,
All our want and sorrow sharing;
God with us, Emmanuel:
Yet, a dearer, closer union
Jesus in His love would frame;
He, the Passover fulfilling,
Gave Himself as Paschal Lamb.
Alleluia, Alleluia
To th'incarnate Son of God,
Who the heav'nly gifts bequeathed us
Of His own true flesh and blood.

The wide variety of terms reflects an even wider variety of understanding of what it is that we are doing. The variations in the interpretations of this ceremony are the source of huge barriers between Christians. For some it is a sacrament, during which something supernatural occurs; to others it is a figurative memorial service.

Likewise there is a difference of opinion as to how often it should be celebrated: for some, as often as possible — the number of performances being of great significance — for the Quakers and the Salvation Army, never. In between there is a bewildering variety of practice — every day, every week, every month, every quarter, every year, etc. If it is a "Passover" as Jesus said, should it be celebrated only once a year on the 14th of Nisan?[2]

> *Then, by man refused and hated,*
> *God for man vouchsafed to die,*
> *Love divine its depth revealing*
> *On the heights of Calvary;*
> *Through His dying the dominion*
> *From the tyrant death was torn,*
> *When its Victim rose its Victor*
> *On the resurrection morn.*
> *Alleluia, Alleluia*
> *To th'incarnate Son of God,*
> *Who through His eternal Spirit*
> *Offers His own flesh and blood.*

---

[2] first month of the Hebrew ecclesiastical calendar

Yet here we are, drawn from many nations, many denominations, and many interpretations. Is there any way that we can celebrate this in the unity of the Spirit? I believe we can, and must. For before us are the elements, bread and wine, whatever our interpretation of their meaning and substance. As we all share in the elements, perhaps we can begin to share in the wide range of truth they show, without losing any truth dear to us. For all interpretations, Jesus is here. It is with Him that we "commune."

Then, adored in highest Heaven,
We shall see the virgin's Son,
All creation bowed before Him,
Man upon th'eternal throne:
Where, like sound of many waters
In one ever rising flood,
Myriad voices hymn His triumph,
Victim, Priest, incarnate God.
Worthy He all praise and blessing
Who, by dying, death o'ercame;
Glory be to God forever!
Alleluia to the Lamb!

JEWISH ROOTS

When we met together previously, I drew our attention to the variety of terms by which this ceremony is known. Today, let us look more closely at what these terms imply.

Although some scholars would argue this point, Jesus called it a "Passover." However great and profound the new significance Jesus gave to it, the term at least surely implies continuity with Jewish faith and practice. What did the Jewish people understand by "Passover?"

The day of resurrection! [3]
Earth, tell it out abroad;
The Passover of gladness,
the Passover of God.
From death to life eternal,
from earth unto the sky,
Our Christ hath brought us over,
with hymns of victory.

---

[3] *The Day of Resurrection*, words by John of Damascus (675-749)

Though it carried a wealth of connotations, let us look just at the main point. The Passover was to serve as a reminder of the salvation that God wrought for the Jews when He delivered them from Egypt. The blood on the door and the meal of the sacrificed lamb reminded them of the price of that redemption when the Angel of Death "passed over" the Israelites.

Our hearts be pure from evil, that we may see aright
The Lord in rays eternal of resurrection light;
And listening to His accents, may hear, so calm and plain,
His own "All hail!" and, hearing, may raise the victor strain.

So too, this our Passover looks back to our salvation, and the body and the blood that purchased it.

As we partake today, let us look back too, recalling the occasion when we were "passed over" by the Angel of Death, and God provided us with our salvation through the blood of our Sacrificial Lamb. — Christ "Our Passover."

Now let the heavens be joyful! Let earth the song begin!
Let the round world keep triumph, and all that is therein!
Let all things seen and unseen their notes in gladness blend,
For Christ the Lord hath risen, our joy that hath no end.

MARRIAGE FEAST

Those who see this ceremony as the "Lord's Table," or the "Lord's Supper," are looking forward in hope to the "Marriage Supper of the Lamb." Jesus Himself said that He would no longer take of the fruit of the vine until He drank it with His disciples in the Kingdom. Paul said we are to do this: "'until He comes." The disciples were not to live in doubt, but in hope.

> *Wake, awake, for night is flying;*[4]
> *The watchmen on the heights are crying:*
> *Awake, Jerusalem, at last!*
> *Midnight hears the welcome voices*
> *And at the thrilling cry rejoices;*
> *Come forth, ye virgins, night is past;*
> *The Bridegroom comes, awake;*
> *Your lamps with gladness take;*
> *Alleluia! And for His marriage feast prepare*
> *For ye must go and meet Him there.*

---

[4] *Wake, Awake, For Night is Flying*, Words by Phillip Nicolai, 1599.

We, too, can look forward to the final culmination of history. The vast confusion of the vicissitudes of existence will all converge to ultimate meaning. Only the Christian worldview gives any possibility of hope. In the New Testament the Greek word (*elpis*) does not carry the weak connotation often associated with the English word "hope," which often means not much more than "wishful thinking." Instead it carries with it a firm expectation, based on trust in the character of the One who made the promise—God—and in His faithfulness to His promises.

> *Zion hears the watchmen singing,*
> *And all her heart with joy is springing;*
> *She wakes, she rises from her gloom;*
> *For her Lord comes down all glorious,*
> *The strong in grace, in truth victorious.*
> *Her Star is risen, her Light is come.*
> *Ah come, Thou blessèd One, God's own belovèd Son:*
> *Alleluia! We follow till the halls we see*
> *Where Thou hast bid us sup with Thee.*

Let us then today, as we partake of the elements, look forward in joyful hope of our final "Supper" at the Marriage Feast of the Lamb, when we will eat with Him in the Kingdom.

Now let all the heavens adore Thee,
And saints and angels sing before Thee,
With harp and cymbal's clearest tone;
Of one pearl each shining portal,
Where we are with the choir immortal
Of angels round Thy dazzling throne;
Nor eye hath seen, nor ear hath yet attained to hear
What there is ours, but we rejoice and sing to Thee
Our hymn of joy eternally.

CELEBRATING
EACH OTHER

If the Passover looks to the past, and the Lord's Supper to the future, those who see the bread and the wine as "Communion" are focusing on the present. The Latin term *communio* has two perspectives: one directed to one another, the other to the Lord Himself. The Greek word is *koinonia* and has the same double significance.

In the first, we are emphasizing our sharing, our community, and our mutual dependence. That is why Paul is so disturbed by the selfishness of the Corinthian Christians who are disgracing the celebration of Communion by eating greedily themselves, and ignoring their destitute brothers and sisters. In Communion we are celebrating each other. I think that perhaps this explains the ambiguity to Paul's words: "not discerning the

Lord's body." Does this refer to Christ's physical body, or to what Paul elsewhere means by the "Body of Christ," that is the Church? Probably both. As we share in this meal, we are communing with each other. We are aware that there are others communing with us.

Of course the deepest communion is with our Lord. In the most daring figure possible, that communion is described as a "feeding on His flesh" and a "drinking of His Blood." Christians have differed in how literally those words are to be interpreted, but all Christians agree on their profound significance. In this ceremony we may enjoy the deepest possible intimacy with our Lord.

Let us therefore now celebrate Communion. Let us take the elements and serve them to each other, to emphasize our sharing in the "Body of Christ." As we do let us also experience the deepest possible intimacy with the Lord who loves us.

Let us break bread together on our knees, (on our knees)[5]
Let us break bread together on our knees. (on our knees)
When I fall on my knees with my face to the rising sun,
    O Lord, have mercy on me.

Let us drink wine together on our knees, (on our knees)
Let us drink wine together on our knees. (on our knees)
When I fall on my knees with my face to the rising sun,
    O Lord, have mercy on me.

Let us praise God together on our knees, (on our knees)
Let us praise God together on our knees. (on our knees)
When I fall on my knees with my face to the rising sun,
    O Lord, have mercy on me.

---

[5] *Let Us Break Bread Together on Our Knees*, African-American spiritual.

TWO JEWS LOOK AT THE LAST SUPPER

Today, let's exercise our imagination and picture ourselves overhearing a conversation between two Jews, Joachim and Ben-Judah, outside the palace of the High Priest where Jesus is being interrogated.

B-J: Joachim, what in the world are you doing here at this hour?

J: Haven't you heard? The Rabbi Jesus was arrested last night, and is now being interrogated by the High Priest. I fear they will find a pretext to kill him.

B-J: Surely not. What fault can they possibly find in Him? In any case God would surely not let anything like that happen to so righteous a man. By the way, didn't He and His disciples celebrate the Passover in your room last night? I think that this must be an honor you will always remember.

J: Oh no, Ben Judah, Oh no. It was a disaster. I will never forget, but I hope no one else ever remembers.

B-J: Good grief! Why? What happened?

J: First of all, no one had made any arrangements for washing their feet. So they had to do it themselves.

B-J: You mean, one of the disciples had to do it?

J: Worse than that. The Master did it!

B-J: Jesus! The Messiah! That is disgraceful! Didn't anyone object?

J: Peter tried to, but Jesus persisted. Then Peter compounded the disgrace by asking the Master to give him a complete bath . . .!

B-J: Good grief! Then what happened?

J: Then the disciples got into a furious argument (which nearly came to blows) as to who was going to have the most prestigious position in the new Messianic Kingdom.

B-J: I suppose the Master settled that by making public what appointments He has in mind.

J: Not at all. Instead, He rebuked them for ambition. He said it was the privilege of His Father to make those appointments. Then He made a statement that was as if He had dropped a huge rock into a pond. "One of those present," He said, "will betray Me." What was disturbing was that none of them denied it, but only anxiously asked, "Is it I?" — as if the thought had in fact crossed their minds. Of course, the one He meant was Judas, who left immediately to do just that. He led the soldiers of the High Priest to where Jesus was in the garden of Gethsemane. Do you see why I hope no one remembers last night? I can just hear it: "Oh yes, that was the night when Jesus had to settle an argument among the 'disciples.' Or, 'the night Jesus had to do the feet washing . . .,' or, God forbid, 'the night He was betrayed…'"

B-J: Did Jesus have any teaching to give?

J: Of course. He had much to say on heaven, the Holy Spirit and so on, but it seems that only John was paying attention.

B-J: What about the actual Passover meal itself? How was the Paschal lamb? I am sure you had provided the very best.

J: No one seems to have noticed it. What everyone remembers are His strange words when He broke the bread and drank one of the Passover cups. "The bread," He said, is "My body, and the wine, My blood." They are already arguing as to how literally they are to take that.

So we can see that even the original "Lord's Supper" was not perfectly conducted. The Lord is not looking for a flawless performance. Nor was it perfect in Corinth. We owe the record of it to its disgraceful nature. So we can see that Christ blesses us, not in perfect performance, but in the reality of our fallen natures. By all means let us examine ourselves, and confess our undeserving, but let us then eat and drink.

I am not worthy, holy Lord,[6]
That Thou shouldst come to me;
Speak but the word; one gracious word
Can set the sinner free.

I am not worthy; cold and bare
The lodging of my soul;
How canst Thou deign to enter there?
Lord, speak, and make me whole.

I am not worthy; yet, my God,
How can I say Thee nay;
Thee, who didst give Thy flesh and blood
My ransom price to pay?

O come! in this sweet morning hour
Feed me with food divine;
And fill with all Thy love and power
This worthless heart of mine.

---

[6] *I Am Not Worthy, Holy Lord*, words by Henry W. Baker, 1875.

A NIGHT OF BETRAYAL

I have often been struck by the strange way in which Paul locates the Last Supper in time. He says, " . . . on the night that Jesus was betrayed . . ." Modern historians would have much preferred some such statement: "On the Wednesday (or Thursday) night of Passion Week." Or, to settle controversy: "on the 12th (or 13th, or 14th) of the month of Nisan.[7]" Sentimentalists might have preferred "on the night on which He told us how much He loved us." Charismatics might prefer "on the night when Jesus promised us His Holy Spirit." But no, it is the betrayal that identifies it in Paul's mind.

Just as I am, without one plea,[8]
But that Thy blood was shed for me,
And that Thou bidst me come to Thee,
O Lamb of God, I come, I come.

---

[7] first month of the Hebrew ecclesiastical calendar

[8] *Just as I Am, Without One Plea*, Words by Charlotte Elliott, 1835

Just as I am, and waiting not
To rid my soul of one dark blot,
To Thee whose blood can cleanse each spot,
O Lamb of God, I come, I come.

It is clear that in the tradition of this Last Supper, what the disciples remembered, what fixed it in their minds was the fact that it was the occasion when Jesus was betrayed — not only by Judas, but to some degree by all of them. In his darkest hour, Judas sold Him, Peter denied knowing Him, and the rest deserted Him and fled in panic.

Just as I am, though tossed about
With many a conflict, many a doubt,
Fightings and fears within, without,
O Lamb of God, I come, I come.

Just as I am, poor, wretched, blind;
Sight, riches, healing of the mind,
Yea, all I need in Thee to find,
O Lamb of God, I come, I come.

All of us, I am sure, can remember occasions when we have betrayed our Lord. Sometimes it was the sudden unprepared-for "fear of man," sometimes the trap of a little white lie. Perhaps not many of us blatantly plan a Judas betrayal. Yet all of us, if we are honest, can think of times, when the love of money, or greed for power, or the lust of the flesh has led us to choose a course of action that honors Mammon more than Christ.

Just as I am, Thou wilt receive,
Wilt welcome, pardon, cleanse, relieve;
Because Thy promise I believe,
O Lamb of God, I come, I come.

Just as I am, Thy love unknown
Hath broken every barrier down;
Now, to be Thine, yea, Thine alone,
O Lamb of God, I come, I come.

What a divine comfort then to realize that Jesus, knowing in advance all the betrayals of the disciples, nonetheless deeply desired to have this Last Supper with them. So let each of us "examine himself" and so eat . . .

Just as I am, of that free love
The breadth, length, depth, and height to prove,
Here for a season, then above,
O Lamb of God, I come, I come!

THE BODY OF CHRIST

I have sometimes thought that the Communion service needs a kind of Surgeon General's warning: "This ceremony may be dangerous to your health; it may, in fact, bring death."

What I am referring to, of course, is Paul's word that because of abuse of the Lord's Supper, some were sick and others were dead.

Though these remarks of Paul's are usually omitted in public celebrations of Communion, we dare not ignore them. It is possible that we too may be guilty of sinning against the body and blood of the Lord, bringing condemnation upon ourselves. It comes from a failure (Paul tells us) to recognize the Body of Christ.

Of course some may wonder: "Just what is meant by recognizing the 'Body of Christ?'" Sacramentalists will no doubt say that it is a failure to realize that the elements of bread and wine have become the very Body and Blood of Christ, in an almost literal sense. Is this what Paul means?

Without dogmatically imposing my view on you, may I share my own interpretation of Paul's meaning? The whole passage is concerned with rebuking the Corinthian church for manifest selfishness where wealthy members were enjoying food and drink while poorer members were going hungry. Either this is a reference to the "Love Feast" which preceded the "Lord's Supper," or the Lord's Supper itself which apparently could consist of far greater portions of the elements, than the purely token portions we are used to.

So it would seem to me that Paul is using the term "Body of Christ," as he does elsewhere, to mean the Church. In that case, the crime would be failure to recognize that your fellow Christian is incarnating Christ, and that to ignore, despise, or exploit him, or her, is to insult Jesus, who said that "whatsoever" things we do to our fellow Christians, good or bad, we are doing to Him.

Let us celebrate "worthily," then, by examining ourselves and then serving the elements to each other.

Behold, how pleasant and how good[9]
That we, one Lord confessing,
Together dwell in brotherhood,
Our unity expressing.
'Tis like the oil on Aaron's head,
The seal of ordination,
That o'er his robes the sweetness shed
Of perfect consecration.
Behold, how pleasant and how good
That we, one Lord confessing,
Together dwell in brotherhood,
Our unity expressing.
'Tis like the dew from Hermon fair
On Zion's hill descending;
The Lord commands His blessing here
In life that is unending.

---

[9]   *Behold, How Pleasant and How Good*, paraphrase of Ps 133, author and date unknown.

TWO CUPS OR FOUR?

I have for some time been puzzled by some aspects of Luke's account of the Last Supper. I am so familiar with Paul's account, which is the one almost universally quoted at celebrations of Communion, that I was startled to read of two cups, one before or during supper, the second after supper.

It was not until I participated in a celebration of a Seder (as the Passover is commonly called among modern Jews) that I began to get some light on the subject.

Apparently in a traditional Seder there are four cups of wine, each with a different significance. The first is the *Kaddish*, which means consecration. The second *Haggadah* which means story, or in some accounts, thanksgiving. The third cup is *Baruch* which means blessing or redemption. And the final cup, *Hallel*, which means praise.

The Apostle Paul calls the cup of Communion the "cup which we bless." This would seem to be the third cup. But what is this first cup of Luke's account? The most satisfactory guess is that it is the second cup of the Passover ceremony, the cup of thanksgiving for all that God has previously done.

This can be the basis on which we understand what Jesus was doing at this point. We learn that after telling the disciples that He would not eat the Passover with them again until the Kingdom of God was fulfilled, He took a cup and gave thanks (Greek *eucharistesas*), then He told the disciples to take it and share it among themselves. I see this as an invitation to share thanksgiving for God's faithfulness in the past. Not only the mighty Red Sea rescues, but also the daily providence of His unfailing provisions. This we are to share with each other.

Those who call the Lord's Supper the "Eucharist" are reflecting this element of the ceremony. Their liturgy begins with thanksgiving. Let us this morning also begin with thanksgiving. May I suggest that we turn to one another and share one thing from our own experience of God's provision and begin our "Eucharist" with thanksgiving . . .

Now thank we all our God, with heart and hands and voices,[10]
Who wondrous things has done, in Whom this world rejoices;
Who from our mothers' arms has blessed us on our way
With countless gifts of love, and still is ours today.

O may this bounteous God through all our life be near us,
With ever joyful hearts and blessèd peace to cheer us;
And keep us in His grace, and guide us when perplexed;
And free us from all ills, in this world and the next!

All praise and thanks to God the Father now be given;
The Son and Him Who reigns with Them in highest Heaven;
The one eternal God, whom earth and Heaven adore;
For thus it was, is now, and shall be evermore.

---

[10] *Now Thank We All Our God*, Martink Rinkart, circa 1936

A LAST SUPPER
EXIT POLL

Have you ever heard of "exit polls?" Journalists trying to gauge how an election is going interview different people as they leave the polling booths to determine how they voted. Let us in our imagination conduct an exit poll on the disciples as they leave the Last Supper, on their way to Gethsemane.

Ah! Here is one. "What is your name, sir, and what do you remember best about the evening?"

Matthew, former Internal Revenue agent. Oh, I was curious as to why Judas left so early and so suddenly, He took the purse with him. I am sure he was up to some mischief. I'm not a tax collector for nothing. I can spot a cheat a mile away. I'll bet he told the Master he was going to give some money to the poor. He'll probably keep it himself.

Simon the Zealot: It was a big disappointment. I thought when He asked if we had a sword, the moment had come when we would rise up and smite the Romans once and for all. Instead He talked about heaven and seemed to imply that He was going to die soon.

Philip: I was totally confused. I just asked the Master for a revelation of God the Father. Instead He said that He was the revelation of the Father. I didn't get the opportunity to follow up on this.

Thomas: He made some incredible claims. Though I love Him and am ready to die for Him, I am going to need some solid evidence that He is who He says He is.

Peter: I am still smarting from His prediction that I will deny Him before the night is out. Well, I have our one and only sword, and I am ready to swing it at anyone who dares touch Him.

John: He said so many wonderful things I am going to have to write them down before I forget. But what I most remember is His giving us a new commandment to put alongside the Ten. Not only must we love God, not only must we love our neighbor, now we have to love one another as well. This is going to be hard when it comes to someone like Judas.

We can imagine that the thoughts of each of the disciples were different as they left the scene of the first Last Supper. I am amazed as we have meditated on it how many different thoughts the scene inspires. Each of us as we leave here will depart with a multitude of different impressions, all in some way linked to the ceremony we are about to make. The common denominator is the fellowship with Jesus, He relates to each one of us where we are.

What a friend we have in Jesus, all our sins and griefs to bear![11]
What a privilege to carry everything to God in prayer!
O what peace we often forfeit, O what needless pain we bear,
All because we do not carry everything to God in prayer.

Have we trials and temptations? Is there trouble anywhere?
We should never be discouraged; take it to the Lord in prayer.
Can we find a friend so faithful who will all our sorrows share?
Jesus knows our every weakness; take it to the Lord in prayer.

Are we weak and heavy laden, cumbered with a load of care?
Precious Savior, still our refuge, take it to the Lord in prayer.
Do your friends despise, forsake you? Take it to the Lord in prayer!
In His arms He'll take and shield you; you will find a solace there.

Blessed Savior, Thou hast promised Thou wilt all our burdens bear
May we ever, Lord, be bringing all to Thee in earnest prayer.
Soon in glory bright unclouded there will be no need for prayer
Rapture, praise and endless worship will be our sweet portion there.

---

[11] *What a Friend We Have in Jesus,* Joseph M. Scriven, 1855

THE FIRST PASSOVER

As we have said: Jesus called the Last Supper a "Passover." Today let us go back to the first Passover and see what it can tell us about this one.

The context is, I am sure, familiar to all. The people of Israel are in bondage to the Egyptians, and eleven plagues have failed to persuade the Pharaoh to let them go. A final plague bringing about the death of the first-born sons is now threatened.

Unlike some of the previous plagues when they were protected simply because they were Israelites, now they were also vulnerable, unless they strictly obeyed the instructions to carry out the Passover meal.

Each man was to provide for his own household, and, if necessary, for his neighbor. He was to choose a male animal, one year old, from either the sheep or the goats, and slaughter it at the same time as all the other Israelites at twilight on the 14th day of the month Nisan.[12] Then they were to take some of the blood and smear it on the posts and lintels of the doors of their houses.

> Eternal, spotless Lamb of God,[13]
> Before the world's foundations slain,
> Sprinkle us ever with Thy blood;
> O cleanse, and keep us ever clean!
> To every soul (all praise to Thee!)
> Our bowels of compassion move;
> And all mankind by this may see
> God is in us; for God is love.

The meat was to be roasted, not eaten raw or boiled. It was to be eaten with bitter herbs and unleavened bread. Nothing was to be left over, and the people were to be dressed, ready to go. Then the angel of Death would pass over.

> Giver and Lord of life, whose power
> And guardian care for all are free,
> To Thee, in fierce temptation's hour,
> From sin and Satan let us flee;
> Thine, Lord, we are, and ours Thou art,
> In us be all Thy goodness showed;
> Renew, enlarge, and fill our heart
> With peace, and joy and Heaven, and God.

---

[12] first month of the Hebrew ecclesiastical calendar
[13] *Eternal, Spotless Lamb of God*, Charles Wesley, 1742.

What can we learn from this for our understanding of Communion? First, I notice that mere membership in the visible body of the people of God was not sufficient in and of itself. Every individual had to follow specific instructions to be saved. He had to share in the sacrifice; he had to be sheltered by the blood on the door. I find the fact that either a lamb or a kid could be used very interesting. A spotless lamb was a symbol of sacrificed innocence, a goat the symbol of guilt. So there is a sense that Jesus is not only the "Lamb of God," but also the "Scapegoat of God" who became Sin for us. We too are not to consider the Supper as a goal in itself, but merely the rally before we go out to meet the world. So we must be dressed for a journey that is to begin when we leave.

> *Blessing and honor, praise and love*
> *Co-equal, co-eternal Three,*
> *In earth below, and Heaven above,*
> *By all Thy works, be paid to Thee!*
> *Thrice Holy! Thine the kingdom is,*
> *The power omnipotent is Thine;*
> *And when created nature dies,*
> *Thy never-ceasing glories shine.*

HEZEKIAH REVIVES THE PASSOVER

In thinking of the Lord's Supper as a "Passover," we have been studying celebrations of the Passover — the first, and then subsequent ones. There are several later ones, such as those connected with revivals of religion under some godly kings, under Hezekiah and Josiah in particular.

Hezekiah, you may recall, was one of the righteous kings of Judah, who sought to restore the pure worship of the Lord in Judah.

As part of this effort he resolved to have a national celebration of the Passover in Jerusalem. We are told that his decision to do so embarrassed the priests who were not ceremoniously "clean" to do the celebrating. Instead of celebrating on the 14th of Nisan[14] when it was supposed to be held, they decided to postpone the event one month.

---

[14] first month of the Hebrew ecclesiastical calendar

Hezekiah then invited one and all, not only from Judah but also from the northern kingdom of Israel. Apparently not many from the northern kingdom accepted the offer, but some did. Alas! They too were ceremoniously unclean. Then Hezekiah did an unusual thing: he prayed to the Lord to permit these "unclean" applicants to take the Passover anyway. And the Lord granted Hezekiah's prayer.

I wonder if it strikes you how unusual this story is. Here we have embarrassed and unprepared priests; a postponement to a month other than the prescribed month is made; worshippers who are ceremoniously "unclean" and from an alien culture partake of the feast. Yet the service goes on, and the Lord brings healing, as the text says.

Yet elsewhere the Lord seems to be very concerned about doing things in the prescribed way. Just think of David, Uzzah, and the ark. How can we reconcile this?

I find a clue in one phrase of Hezekiah's prayer. ". . . may the Lord pardon those who have set their heart on seeking God."

God is more interested in sincere seekers, than in perfect protocol. Perhaps some of us are aware that we do not come to the Lord's Table "ceremoniously clean," or spiritually fit. Perhaps we need to pray Hezekiah's prayer for ourselves, and receive the healing that Hezekiah's worshippers received.

⁂

Search me, O God,[15]
And know my heart today;
Try me, O Savior,
Know my thoughts, I pray.
See if there be
Some wicked way in me;
Cleanse me from every sin
And set me free.

I praise Thee, Lord,
For cleansing me from sin;
Fulfill Thy Word,
And make me pure within.
Fill me with fire
Where once I burned with shame;
Grant my desire
To magnify Thy Name.

---

[15] *Search Me, O God*, J. Edwin Orr, 1936

Lord, take my life,
And make it wholly Thine;
Fill my poor heart
With Thy great love divine.
Take all my will,
My passion, self and pride;
I now surrender, Lord
In me abide.

O Holy Ghost,
Revival comes from Thee;
Send a revival,
Start the work in me.
Thy Word declares
Thou wilt supply our need;
For blessings now,
O Lord, I humbly plead.

FOOT WASHING

John's account of the Last Supper begins with the description of the foot washing. A few Christian groups have continued the practice as a ritual, either as part of Communion or separately, but by and large it has been not imitated in Christian circles. On a few occasions we have included a foot washing in our celebrations of Communion.

Whether or not we retain it as a ritual ceremony, we cannot afford to miss its lessons for our own communing in the Eucharist.

> *Forever here my rest shall be,*[16]
> *Close to Thy bleeding side;*
> *This all my hope, and all my plea,*
> *For me the Savior died!*

---

[16] *Forever Here My Rest Shall Be*, Charles Wesley, 1740

First of all is the lesson that our "feet need washing." We come to the Lord's Table with our feet filthy with the muck and mire of the world.

> *My dying Savior, and my God,*
> *Fountain for guilt and sin,*
> *Sprinkle me ever in Thy blood,*
> *And cleanse, and keep me clean.*

Second, only the Lord can do the washing. Furthermore He does not do just a vague general washing, but zeroes in on the specific need of the moment. God is a God of specifics. He does so, whether we understand what is going on or not. Peter would not understand until later. Jesus pointed out that this specific washing of our feet is all that is needed if we have previously been washed all over and are otherwise "clean."

> *Wash me, and make me thus Thine own,*
> *Wash me, and mine Thou art,*
> *Wash me, but not my feet alone,*
> *My hands, my head, my heart.*

Thirdly, true leadership is one of service and humility, a surrender of the "rights" of "Teacher" or "Leader."

Lastly, we are to follow this example of servant leadership by imitating our Leader.

> *The atonement of Thy blood apply,*
> *Till faith to sight improve,*
> *Till hope shall in fruition die,*
> *And all my soul be love.*

Let us this morning allow Jesus to wash our feet if they are "dirty;" our hands if they are "bloody;" our heads if they are full of impurity. Then let us wash one another's feet. Let us lead by serving. Finally, let us "examine ourselves" and so eat of the feast.

> *I do believe, I now believe,*
> *That Jesus died for me;*
> *And through His blood, His precious blood,*
> *I shall from sin be free.*

TWO KINDS OF NIGHT

In a way it is somewhat surprising that John makes the comment when Judas went out that "It was night." It might be simply a chronological notice: it was the most important day in history, which would begin according to Jewish reckoning after sunset. It was the very day that Christ was crucified.

When the rest of the disciples and Jesus left a little later, the account simply says: "After they had sung a hymn, they went out to the Mount of Olives." It seems that on the walk to Gethsemane, Jesus continued to teach and rebuke them. It may have been night, but they were still in fellowship.

I can't help thinking, however, that with Judas the remark is symbolic. It was not a night of starlight, such as is common in the Middle East, but rather the deep, dark night of sin and a betrayer's heart.

We have the choice: All of us go out into a night: a night of betrayal or a night of continued fellowship with the Master.

<center>~~~</center>

All praise to Thee, my God, this night,[17]
For all the blessings of the light!
Keep me, O keep me, King of kings,
Beneath Thine own almighty wings.

Forgive me, Lord, for Thy dear Son,
The ill that I this day have done,
That with the world, myself, and Thee,
I, ere I sleep, at peace may be.

Teach me to live, that I may dread
The grave as little as my bed.
Teach me to die, that so I may
Rise glorious at the judgment day.

O may my soul on Thee repose,
And with sweet sleep mine eyelids close,
Sleep that may me more vigorous make
To serve my God when I awake.

---

[17] *All Praise to Thee, My God, This Night*, Thomas Ken, circa 1674

When in the night I sleepless lie,
My soul with heavenly thoughts supply;
Let no ill dreams disturb my rest,
No powers of darkness me molest.

O when shall I, in endless day,
For ever chase dark sleep away,
And hymns divine with angels sing,
All praise to thee, eternal King?

Praise God, from Whom all blessings flow;
Praise Him, all creatures here below;
Praise Him above, ye heavenly host;
Praise Father, Son, and Holy Ghost.

OUR PAST, OUR PRESENT, OUR FUTURE

When we look at John's account of the Last Supper, we cannot help but be struck by the great difference between his account and those of the Synoptic Gospels. He alone has the story of the foot washing, and he alone gives the substance of Jesus's message on that occasion. On the other hand, he alone omits the institution of the Bread and Wine.

In fact the message in John 14 to 17 has always seemed to me to be totally detached from the Last Supper, something of general application but not very relevant to the immediate context. But as I was meditating on these chapters it suddenly came to me that there was a connection, subtle, but nonetheless real . . . and significant.

You will recall that we have seen that the Lord's Supper has a triple focus: as a "Passover" it looks back at our salvation; as "Communion" it looks at our present fellowship with our Lord and each other; as the "Lord's Supper" it looks forward to the final consummation of the Marriage Supper of the Lamb.

As I looked at the chapters in John it became apparent to me that these three foci were to be found there too, but in reverse order. "Let not your heart be troubled," He begins, showing the Lord's Table as a pledge of heaven, in which Who He Is as the Way to the Father guarantees us our blessed Hope. Then He speaks of "the Other Comforter," the Holy Spirit, and the image of the vine and the branches, both of which speaks of the Communion of His present Presence. Finally in His High Priestly prayer in chapter 17, He rejoices with His Father over the salvation of those whom the Father has given Him, our Passover.

As we partake of the elements today, let us enrich our spirits and minds by meditating on those precious words in John — our salvation, our present communion, and our future hope . . .

My hope is built on nothing less[18]
Than Jesus's blood and righteousness.
I dare not trust the sweetest frame,
But wholly trust in Jesus's Name.

On Christ the solid Rock I stand,
All other ground is sinking sand;
All other ground is sinking sand.

When darkness seems to hide His face,
I rest on His unchanging grace.
In every high and stormy gale,
My anchor holds within the veil.

His oath, His covenant, His blood,
Support me in the whelming flood.
When all around my soul gives way,
He then is all my Hope and Stay

When He shall come with trumpet sound,
Oh may I then in Him be found.
Dressed in His righteousness alone,
Faultless to stand before the throne.

---

[18] *My Hope is Built on Nothing Less*, Edward Mote, circa 1834.

HIGH AND LOW
CHURCH

I'll never forget the first Communion service I witnessed in our Presbyterian church in Bethlehem, PA. I have never seen such carefully choreographed movements on the part of the distinguished elders who served. They were all dressed alike in "morning coats" and wore identical carnations in their buttonholes. They marched in impeccable lock step, and moved from row to row in perfect harmony. The mood was of perfect solemnity.

I was reminded of this, (alas, in contrast!) at our most recent communion service when those who served were dressed in every degree of casual attire imaginable, from grunge to graciosa. We ran out of communion cups and had to serve the last group with paper cups. Worst of all, the prayer of consecration was offered, not by an "ordained" clergyman, but by me, an unordained layman. Was our service valid? Did we in fact, "commune?"

It would be a great mistake to decide too quickly that either impeccable protocol or sloppy casualness is acceptable. The former can far too easily slip into an arid ritualism that falls into the *ex opera operata* heresy; that is, the doctrine that as long as the right words are said by the right person, a valid communion has occurred. The latter demonstrates that the ceremony is not being taken seriously. After all if the groom shows up at the wedding in dirty shorts and tee shirt, the bride might well wonder how committed he was going to be. This is what lies behind New Testament references to guests being excluded from weddings because they did not wear an appropriate wedding garment.

But the New Testament makes it clear that it is not "attire" but "attitude" which is important. However it remains true that attire is often an indicator of attitude. The attitude of the Corinthian church — one of self-centered disunity — led to sickness and death. We are to examine ourselves, not for ritualistic perfection, nor for flippant casualness (though each may betray a deeper problem), but for our attitude of indifference to our brother and sister, or our blindness to the Presence of the Lord.

Paul makes it clear that some intended "Lord's Suppers" were not in fact "Lord's Suppers" at all. He says in 1 Corinthians 11:20: "When you come together it is not the Lord's Supper that you eat." The problem with the Corinthians was not protocol, but attitude. By their selfishness, greed and lack of compassion for the poorer members of the body, they were making a farce of the "Communion," and celebrating in its stead "Division."

We need to look over the group of people here and see if there are any you are looking down upon, thus excluding from fellowship with you. If so, before you participate go to that person and make it right.

In Christ there is no East or West,[19]
In Him no South or North;
But one great fellowship of love
Throughout the whole wide earth.

In Him shall true hearts everywhere
Their high communion find;
His service is the golden cord,
Close binding humankind.

Join hands, then, members of the faith,
Whate'er your race may be!
Who serves my Father as His child
Is surely kin to me.

In Christ now meet both East and West,
In Him meet North and South;
All Christly souls are one in Him
Throughout the whole wide earth.

---

[19] *In Christ There is No East or West*, William A. Dunkerley, 1908.

BELIEVING IN JESUS

As Jesus opens His discourse, He begins with reassurance: "Let not your heart be troubled . . ." Because of an ambiguity in Greek grammar, it is not clear whether His next comment is a statement or a command: "Believe in God, believe also in Me" or "You believe in God [already], believe in Me." I have my own private rule of interpretation: whenever the Greek can be translated legitimately in several ways, all are significant.

Thus it is that at our celebration of this ceremony we too face the same command and the same statement. There is a sense in which nearly everybody believes in God, or at least claims to. But "believing in" means much more than "believing that" someone exists: it means committing oneself to that person. So Jesus is making the stupendous claim to the same commitment we owe to God.

If it is a command, we can see that our commitment to Jesus is on the same level as our obligation to believe in God. So it is that our participation in the Communion, among other things, is a recommitment of faith in the Savior and His Father together.

Jesus shall reign where'er the sun[20]
Does his successive journeys run;
His kingdom stretch from shore to shore,
Till moons shall wax and wane no more.

People and realms of every tongue
Dwell on His love with sweetest song;
And infant voices shall proclaim
Their early blessings on His Name.

Blessings abound where'er He reigns;
The prisoner leaps to lose his chains;
The weary find eternal rest,
And all the sons of want are blessed.

---

[20] *Jesus Shall Reign Where'er the Sun*, Isaac Watts, 1719. Selected verses.

Let every creature rise and bring
Peculiar honors to our King;
Angels descend with songs again,
And earth repeat the loud amen!

Great God, whose universal sway
The known and unknown worlds obey,
Now give the kingdom to Thy Son,
Extend His power, exalt His throne.

The scepter well becomes His hands;
All Heav'n submits to His commands;
His justice shall avenge the poor,
And pride and rage prevail no more.

The saints shall flourish in His days,
Dressed in the robes of joy and praise;
Peace, like a river, from His throne
Shall flow to nations yet unknown.

THE HOLY SPIRIT'S ROLE IN COMMUNION

We don't normally think of the Holy Spirit in connection with Communion. But some of the most precious promises referring to Him were uttered by Jesus during His talk at the Last Supper. They are found in John 14 and 16. Let us look at a few of these truths in the light of the fact that they were revealed at the Last Supper.

In His first reference (John 14:25), Jesus promised that the Father would send "another Comforter," that is, a comforter like the comforter they already knew, Jesus Himself. This promise is to be the basis of the peace that Jesus would give, and the hope of His return, and a demonstration of His relationship with the Father.

Spirit of God, descend upon my heart;[21]
Wean it from earth; through all its pulses move;
Stoop to my weakness, mighty as Thou art;
And make me love Thee as I ought to love.

I ask no dream, no prophet ecstasies,
No sudden rending of the veil of clay,
No angel visitant, no opening skies;
But take the dimness of my soul away.

The second passage (John 16:7ff), discusses in more detail the work of the Spirit. Here He is sent by Jesus, and He (*ekeinos*, "that one," masculine) will convict the world of sin for not believing in Christ, of the righteousness of Jesus because He was validated by His ascension and of the nature of the final judgment, since Satan is condemned. He then goes on to say that the Spirit will not speak of Himself, but of Jesus's words and deeds . . .in this way leading us into all truth.

Teach me to feel that Thou art always nigh;
Teach me the struggles of the soul to bear.
To check the rising doubt, the rebel sigh,
Teach me the patience of unanswered prayer.

---

21 *Spirit of God, Descend Upon My Heart*, George Croly, 1854.

But how are these truths relevant to the Communion service? I am not sure that I begin to understand all that is implied, but one truth comes to me. As we partake of these elements, it is the Holy Spirit who is the active agent in ministering Christ's life to us. It is His characteristic office to remind us of Jesus, both His words and deeds. He is not merely interested in giving us an "experience," He wants to bring us to an awareness of truth. The Lord's Supper is to show forth His death, until He comes. It will be the Holy Spirit who makes this ceremony effective as a declaration of Jesus's work.

Hast Thou not bid me love Thee, God and King?
All, all Thine own, soul, heart and strength and mind.
I see Thy cross; there teach my heart to cling:
O let me seek Thee, and O let me find!

Teach me to love Thee as Thine angels love,
One holy passion filling all my frame;
The kindling of the heaven descended Dove,
My heart an altar, and Thy love the flame.

JESUS'S PRAYER FOR US

John's account of the Last Supper ends with the real "Lord's Prayer." What we usually call the "Lord's Prayer," should be called the "Disciples' Prayer" since it is what we should pray. But in John 17 we have the incredible privilege of listening in to our Lord praying to His Father. And we discover that He is praying for us! It is intercessory prayer.

There is not time today to do more than look at a few of the treasures in this prayer. Jesus thanks the Father for being given us, the believers. Later, He mentions that we believers belonged to God even before we acknowledged that Lordship, and that the Father gave us to Jesus, so that now we know that what Jesus is and does and teaches is of God.

He then promises to continue to pray for them… not only the original disciples, but also for those who will believe because of their testimony. That's us! Jesus is now praying for us.

Lord, who the night You were betrayed did pray[22]
That all Your Church might be forever one;
Help us at every Eucharist to say
With willing heart and soul, "Your will be done."
That we may all one bread, one body be
Through this, Your sacrament of unity.

For all Your Church on earth, we intercede;
Lord, make our sad divisions soon to cease;
Draw us all closer, each to each, we plead,
By drawing all to You, O Prince of Peace;
So may we all one bread, one body be,
Through this blest sacrament of unity.

And hear our prayer for wanderers from Your fold;
Restore them, too, Good Shepherd of the sheep,
Back to the faith your saints confessed of old,
And to the Church still pledged that faith to keep.
Soon may we all one bread, one body be,
Through this blest sacrament of unity.

So, Lord, at length when sacraments shall cease,
May we be one with all your Church above—
One with Your saints in one unbroken peace,
One as Your bride in one unbounded love;
More blessed still, in peace and love to be
One with the Trinity in unity.

---

[22] *Lord, Who the Night You Were Betrayed*, Words by William H. Turton, 1881

LORD'S SUPPER AS PROCLAMATION

The two sacraments, Baptism and the Lord's Supper, are both little dramas, in which are enacted various aspects of the Gospel. They have a purpose beyond the edification of the believer. They are a form of Proclamation and should display to the world aspects of the truth of the Good News. Baptism portrays our identification with Christ in His death, burial and resurrection. We die to sin, are buried with Him but rise again to newness of life.

Just what are we proclaiming as we partake of the element of the Lord's Supper? First of all we are proclaiming the Death of Christ. Not only that Jesus died, but that His Death was "for us." His body was "broken for us." Furthermore, we are showing that we appropriate the benefits of that Death by "feeding on Him." All of this sees an ultimate fulfillment in the future "until He comes . . ."

Secondly, we are proclaiming that, as a necessary corollary, we do the feeding in company with others — the "Body of Christ." It is a "communion." That is why the selfishness displayed by the wealthy Corinthians was so abhorrent: They were no longer partaking of the Lord's Supper because they failed to "discern the Lord's Body."

Finally, we are expressing a Hope: "until He comes" rings in our ears. This meal is a preliminary, the *hors d'oeuvres* as it were, of the great feast, which He will once again eat with us. In the words of the folk-hymn "…we'll understand it all bye and bye."

O for a thousand tongues to sing[23]
My great Redeemer's praise,
The glories of my God and King,
The triumphs of His grace!

My gracious Master and my God,
Assist me to proclaim,
To spread through all the earth abroad
The honors of Thy name.

Jesus! the name that charms our fears,
That bids our sorrows cease;
'Tis music in the sinner's ears,
'Tis life, and health, and peace.

He breaks the power of canceled sin,
He sets the prisoner free;
His blood can make the foulest clean,
His blood availed for me.

Hear Him, ye deaf; His praise, ye dumb,
Your loosened tongues employ;
Ye blind, behold your Savior come,
And leap, ye lame, for joy.

See all your sins on Jesus laid:
The Lamb of God was slain,
His soul was once an offering made
For every soul of man.

---

23   *O For a Thousand Tongues to Sing*, Charles Wesley, 1739. Selected verses.

"THE LORD'S BREAKFAST?"

When I was a naughty little boy, during Communion services I used to snicker together with my friend about the term "The Lord's Supper." It was invariably being celebrated in the morning, and we used to say that it should be called "the Lord's Breakfast." Something triggered my memory of those childish peccadilloes, and reminded me that only a few days after the Last Supper, Jesus did serve a breakfast. It was beside the Sea of Galilee. The disciples had returned to their former occupation of fishing. They fished all night but caught nothing. Then Jesus appeared on the shore and calling to them as "children," told them to cast their nets on the opposite side of the boat. Thereupon they caught a huge draught of fish. Peter, recognizing Jesus, wrapped himself in his fisherman's coat and jumped into the sea, (swimming, not walking on the water as once before) and found Jesus with a fire laid and provisions of bread and fish.

Is there any connection of this breakfast with the Last Supper, apart from the apparent fact that this was His first meal with them since then? (I assume that He did not finish the meal with the two on their way to Emmaus.) It was when I considered the interview with Peter after the meal that I saw a connection. As we all know, Jesus took this opportunity to be reconciled to Peter. Twice He asked Peter whether he loved Him or not, using the word *agape* for unconditional love. Twice Peter replied that he did love Him (using the word *phileo,* or friendship love). Thereupon Jesus gave Peter an assignment to "Feed His Sheep." Finally a third time Jesus asked him again, this time using Peter's word for love. When Peter vehemently asserts that he does, Jesus gives him his assignment once again.

First of all, the question asked three times, harked back to the three times that Peter had denied his Lord, as Jesus had prophesied at the Last Supper. His was a triple sin, a triple forgiveness and a triple assignment to a ministry.

Finally, Jesus takes this opportunity to prophesy that Peter too would die on a cross. This should remind us that the Lord's Supper not only signifies Jesus's death, but also that we too have a cross, a death to die. Let us take up our crosses and follow Him.

⚜

"Take up thy cross," the Savior said,[24]
"If thou wouldst My disciple be;
Deny thyself, the world forsake,
And humbly follow after Me."

Take up thy cross, let not its weight
Fill thy weak spirit with alarm;
His strength shall bear thy spirit up,
And brace thy heart and nerve thine arm.

Take up thy cross, nor heed the shame,
Nor let thy foolish pride rebel;
Thy Lord for thee the cross endured,
And saved thy soul from death and hell.

Take up thy cross then in His strength,
And calmly sin's wild deluge brave,
'Twill guide thee to a better home,
It points to glory o'er the grave.

---

[24] *Take Up Thy Cross*, Charles W. Everest, 1833

Take up thy cross and follow Christ,
Nor think till death to lay it down;
For only those who bear the cross
May hope to wear the glorious crown.

To Thee, great Lord, the One in Three,
All praise forevermore ascend:
O grant us in our home to see
The heavenly life that knows no end.

ALMOST OBSESSIVE DESIRE

One day as I was reading Luke's account of the Last Supper in Greek, I was struck by an expression that seemed a rather non-Greek way of saying things, but fully in accord with Semitic grammar. Literally He says: "With desire I have desired to eat this Passover..." This would be the way that in Aramaic one might say: "I have exceedingly desired . . ." emphasizing the extreme intensity of that desire. The English translations somehow miss the urgency.

Furthermore I was struck also by the word itself, *epithumia*, which is a very strong word, in most contexts meaning "lust." It could almost be translated here as signifying: " I have an almost obsessive desire to . . ." I wanted to ask: "Why this intensity? It is clear that the Lord attached tremendous importance to this event, even though He knew ahead of time that the disciples were not really ready and were going to spoil the occasion by arguments and eventually, betrayal.

Do we realize how deeply the Lord wants us to join Him at His table today? This is no casual ritual. It is the call of our Lover to a tryst.

❦

O the deep, deep love of Jesus, vast, unmeasured, boundless, free![25]
Rolling as a mighty ocean in its fullness over me!
Underneath me, all around me, is the current of Thy love
Leading onward, leading homeward to Thy glorious rest above!

O the deep, deep love of Jesus, spread His praise from shore to shore!
How He loveth, ever loveth, changeth never, nevermore!
How He watches o'er His loved ones, died to call them all His own;
How for them He intercedeth, watcheth o'er them from the throne!

O the deep, deep love of Jesus, love of every love the best!
'Tis an ocean full of blessing, 'tis a haven giving rest!
O the deep, deep love of Jesus, 'tis a heaven of heavens to me;
And it lifts me up to glory, for it lifts me up to Thee!

---

[25] *O, the Deep, Deep Love of Jesus*, S. Trevor Francis, 1875.

THE MISSING LAMB

There is a story by Conan Doyle where the famous detective Sherlock Holmes solves a mystery, not through a clue, but through the absence of a clue. The mystery was solved because of a dog that did not bark.

There is a deep mystery at the heart of the Lord's Supper, and a clue that unlocks it is something that is not there. I am referring to the amazing fact that in none of the accounts of the actual Last Supper, in the four Gospels or in Corinthians, is there a reference to the central element of a Passover meal; that is, eating the Passover lamb. It is true that in introducing the account, Matthew, Mark, and Luke explain that the Passover is when the lamb was to be sacrificed, but do not mention it again. John omits all reference to it.

The Passover lamb was the object of very careful, explicit, and complicated instructions.

Its choice, its slaughtering, its cooking, its eating, and its disposal were described in great detail in Exodus. It is the central element in the ceremony, but not in the New Testament accounts. The bread and the cups of wine are described, but not the lamb. Why?

When we think about it, the explanation is obvious — Jesus Himself is the Passover lamb. In an earlier chapter in John, Jesus speaks of eating His flesh and drinking His blood. Though He goes on to say that it is His words that give life, not the flesh, there are many Christians who apply that concept to the participation in the Lord's Supper.

Whether we interpret the feeding on Him spiritually or literally, all agree that we are participating in the life of Christ in the most intimate possible way.

❦

> *The Lamb's high banquet called to share,*[26]
> *Arrayed in garments white and fair,*
> *The Red Sea past, we fain would sing*
> *To Jesus our triumphant King.*

---

[26] *The Lamb's High Banquet Called To Share*, Unknown author. Translated from Latin to English by John M. Neale (1818-1866)

Upon the altar of the cross
His body hath redeemed our loss;
And, tasting of His precious blood,
Our life is hid with Him in God.

Protected in the Paschal night
From the destroying angel's might,
In triumph went the ransomed free
From Pharaoh's cruel tyranny.

Now Christ our Passover is slain,
The Lamb of God without a stain;
His flesh, the true unleavened Bread,
Is freely offered in our stead.

O all sufficient Sacrifice,
Beneath Thee hell defeated lies;
Thy captive people are set free,
And crowns of life restored by Thee.

We hymn Thee rising from the grave,
From death returning, strong to save;
Thine own right hand the tyrant chains,
And Paradise for man regains.

All praise be Thine, O risen Lord,
From death to endless life restored;
All praise to God the Father be
And Holy Ghost eternally.

BREAKING OF BREAD

In the course of describing the Last Supper the writers describe Jesus taking a loaf of bread, giving thanks, and then breaking it. Let us meditate for a few moments on the significance of this phrase: "breaking bread."

> *Break Thou the bread of life, dear Lord, to me,*[27]
> *As Thou didst break the loaves beside the sea;*
> *Beyond the sacred page I seek Thee, Lord;*
> *My spirit pants for Thee, O living Word!*

The phrase is commonly used to describe the taking of a regular meal, and this may be its significance in Acts, where we are told that the believers met from house to house, "breaking bread." On the other hand, it is possible, even likely, that the reference is to celebrations of the

---

[27] *Break Thou the Bread of Life*, Mary A. Lathbury, 1877.

Lord's Supper. It was the act of "breaking bread" that revealed Christ to the disciples at Emmaus on Resurrection Day. And countless commentators since that time have seen in that phrase a reference to Communion.

> *Bless Thou the truth, dear Lord, to me, to me,*
> *As Thou didst bless the bread by Galilee;*
> *Then shall all bondage cease, all fetters fall;*
> *And I shall find my peace, my all in all.*

Even so, I would like to dwell for a minute on the ordinary significance of the expression. We are so used to celebrating Communion in a sacred atmosphere: Immaculate linen, highly ornate serving dishes, stirring music, and so forth, that we miss one of the elements of the Passover: it was a family affair. It was celebrated at home with the common food and drink of everyday living. Bread and wine. Breaking the loaf of bread was the normal way to begin to serve it. Jesus was taking the ordinary and giving it transformed meaning and sublime significance. It is just possible that He intended the Lord's Supper to be celebrated at home, at an ordinary meal, not in a church service.

Thou art the bread of life, O Lord, to me,
Thy holy Word the truth that saveth me;
Give me to eat and live with Thee above;
Teach me to love Thy truth, for Thou art love.

Thus the common ordinary broken bread becomes the symbol of the broken Body of Christ. Is that not what Christ does to the ordinary in our lives? Would you allow the Lord to transform the commonplace in your life by giving it transcendent meaning?

O send Thy Spirit, Lord, now unto me,
That He may touch my eyes, and make me see:
Show me the truth concealed within Thy Word,
And in Thy Book revealed I see the Lord.

CUP OF THE NEW COVENANT

I had a dear friend once, now in Glory, who as a fellow archaeological student tramped around the Near East with me, examining ancient sites. He was an ordained Lutheran minister, and it was inevitable that some of our discussions centered on our differing perceptions of the Lord's Supper. He was a firm believer in the Lutheran doctrine of "consubstantiation" (which states that the Body of Christ is physically present "under the elements of the bread and wine.") To prove that, he quoted Jesus's words, "This is My Body."

I then asked him about the "Cup." Instead of saying of the wine: "This is My blood," Jesus says: "This cup is the New Testament in My Blood." In other words, He did not indicate a literal connection of the wine and His blood. I forget my friend's answer to that, but he had one I am sure.

I am not telling this story to score points in a controversy that goes back, I believe, to the very first celebration of the Last Supper itself. Much less do I think that my personal opinion can settle an argument that has been in the church since Day One. Jesus was always having trouble with those who inappropriately took His words literally. Nicodemus wanted to know if to be "born again" he would have to reenter his mother's womb. On the other hand, He had equal trouble with those who took His literal words too figuratively. His disciples refused to believe that He would be literally crucified, die and rise again on the third day. All of us are in the presence of mystery.

What saddened me most about that situation was the conviction of my friend that because we disagreed on the significance of the ceremony, we could not share it. We shared many a journey, many a hardship, many an experience, many a time of worship, but from his viewpoint, we couldn't share Communion.

It is my prayer this morning, no matter how divergent may be our understanding of the meaning of this ceremony, that we can share it together, and perhaps share our differing perspectives to bless each other.

Come and let us sweetly join,[28]
Christ to praise in hymns divine;
Give we all with one accord
Glory to our common Lord.

Plant in us Thy humble mind;
Patient, pitiful, and kind,
Meek and lowly let us be,
Full of goodness, full of Thee.

Jesus, dear expected guest,
Thou art bidden to the feast,
For Thyself our hearts prepare,
Come, and sit, and banquet there!

Sanctify us, Lord, and bless,
Breathe Thy Spirit, give Thy peace,
Thou Thyself within us move,
Make our feast a feast of love.

Call, O call us each by name,
To the marriage of the Lamb;
Let us lean upon Thy breast,
Love be there our endless feast!

While we walk with God in light,
God our hearts doth still unite;
Dearest fellowship we prove,
Fellowship in Jesus's love.

---

[28] *Come And Let Us Sweetly Join*, Charles Wesley, 1740. Selected verses.

Sweetly each, with each combined,
In the bonds of duty joined,
Feels the cleansing blood applied,
Daily feels that Christ hath died.

Hence may all our actions flow,
Love the proof that Christ we know;
Mutual love the token be,
Lord, that we belong to Thee

Love, Thine image, love impart!
Stamp it on our face and heart!
Only love to us be given!
Lord, we ask no other heaven.

A Cup of Thanksgiving

As I have noted on an earlier occasion, Luke alone mentions an earlier cup of wine drunk during the meal, while the cup of Communion is drunk "after supper." I suggested that this may be one of the four cups which were drunk at the Passover meal. If so, it was probably the second cup called *Haggadhah* which means "story," because at this point the story of the Exodus and the first Passover was told. Because the relating of the story evoked a response of thanksgiving, the cup is also known as the "cup of Thanksgiving," which in the Greek would be *Eucharistia*.

So those who call this ceremony the "Eucharist" are reflecting this aspect of its meaning. It is a joyful celebration, not a doleful ritual. It is to proclaim with joy and genuine thankfulness the reality of the wonderful grace of God.

So it is appropriate to call our participation in this ceremony a "celebration" of the "Eucharist." Singing and even dancing are called for, even though the subject is the sacrificial death of our Lord.

∾

Hosanna in the highest[29]
To our exalted Savior,
Who left behind for all mankind
These tokens of His favor:
His bleeding love and mercy,
His all redeeming Passion;
Who here displays, and gives the grace
Which brings us our salvation.

Angels in fixed amazement
Around our altars hover,
With eager gaze adore the grace
Of our eternal Lover:
Himself and all His fullness
Who gives to the believer;
And by this bread whoe'er are fed
Shall live with God for ever.

---

[29] *Hosanna in the Highest*, Charles Wesley, 1745. Selected verses.

"And When They Had Sung a Hymn..."

G iven the enormous emphasis that we give to music of all kinds in our contemporary worship scene, it comes as a surprise to realize that this is the only occasion on which we are explicitly told that Jesus sang anything.

If the commentators are right, what Jesus and His disciples sang at this first "Lord's Supper" was the sequence of Psalms from 115 to 118. This was the traditional practice during the Passover celebrations.

As I thought about this, I began to wonder what would have been the themes of the music sung at that first Communion?

Psalm 115 begins with the declaration: "Not to us, O Lord, not to us, but to your Name be the glory . . ." It goes on to contrast the impotence of heathen idols to the power and love of the Lord who remembers us and will bless us. Psalm 116 thanks the Lord for His deliverance from certain death. "When I was in great need He saved me." Psalm 117 is a very short burst of praise for God's faithfulness to all nations. Psalm 118 is a song of rejoicing for God's protection in the face of enemies. The Psalmist says: "This is the day that the Lord has made, let us rejoice and be glad in it."

That last verse has been set to music. Why don't we sing it too on this our Passover celebration of God's deliverance?

This is the day the Lord hath made;[30]
He calls the hours His own;
Let Heav'n rejoice, let earth be glad,
And praise surround the throne.

Today He rose and left the dead,
And Satan's empire fell;
Today the saints His triumphs spread,
And all His wonders tell.

Hosanna to th'anointed King,
To David's holy Son;
Help us, O Lord; descend and bring
Salvation from Thy throne.

---

30 *This is the Day the Lord Hath Made*, Isaac Watts, 1719.

Blest be the Lord, who comes to men
With messages of grace;
Who comes in God His Father's Name,
To save our sinful race.

Hosanna in the highest strains
The Church on earth can raise;
The highest heav'ns, in which He reigns,
Shall give Him nobler praise.

About the Author

Douglas D. Feaver was born in 1921 in Toronto, Ontario as the only son of Charles and Margaret Feaver. He earned his B.A. in Greek at the University of Toronto and his Ph.D. in Classics from Johns Hopkins, Baltimore, MD.

Dr. Feaver served for two years as an assistant professor in Classics at Yale University in New Haven, CT, then for over three decades as a professor of Classics at Lehigh University in Bethlehem, PA.

Douglas and his wife Margaret served with Youth With A Mission (YWAM) for 15 years in Kona, HI. Dr. Feaver's role as founding dean of the College of Humanities and International Studies proved to be formative for YWAM's University of the Nations as a whole.

His wife, Margaret Feaver, has published a book called *Precious Pearls: An Inheritance of Tears and Treasures*, recounting lessons from her life experiences as a young woman, wife and mother.

Douglas and Margaret Feaver live in Bethlehem, PA. They have four sons, of whom three are still living: David, in Allentown, PA; John in Oakhurst, NJ, and Peter in Durham, NC. Their daughter Ruth is their next-door neighbor in Bethlehem.